SCRAPES WITH SNAKES!

True Stories of Adventures With Animals

Brady Barr
With Kathleen Weidner Zoehfeld

NATIONAL
GEOGRAPHIC

WASHINGTON, D.C.

The National Geographic Society is
one of the world's largest nonprofit
scientific and educational
organizations. Founded in 1888
to "increase and diffuse
geographic knowledge," the
Society's mission is to inspire people
to care about the planet. It reaches more than 400
million people worldwide each month through its
official journal, *National Geographic,* and other
magazines; National Geographic Channel; television
documentaries; music; radio; films; books; DVDs;
maps; exhibitions; live events; school publishing
programs; interactive media; and merchandise.
National Geographic has funded more than 10,000
scientific research, conservation, and exploration
projects and supports an education program
promoting geographic literacy.

Published by the
National Geographic Society

Gary E. Knell, *President and
    Chief Executive Officer*
John M. Fahey, *Chairman of the Board*
Declan Moore, *Executive Vice President;
    President, Publishing and Travel*
Melina Gerosa Bellows, *Publisher and Chief
    Creative Officer, Books, Kids, and Family*

Prepared by the Book Division
Hector Sierra, *Senior Vice President and
    General Manager*
Nancy Laties Feresten, *Senior Vice President,
    Kids Publishing and Media*
Jennifer Emmett, *Vice President,
    Editorial Director, Kids Books*
Eva Absher-Schantz, *Design Director,
    Kids Publishing and Media*
Jay Sumner, *Director of Photography,
    Kids Publishing*
R. Gary Colbert, *Production Director*
Jennifer A. Thornton, *Director of Managing
    Editorial*

Staff for This Book
Shelby Alinsky, *Project Editor*
Hillary Leo, *Photo Editor*
Callie Broaddus, *Art Director*
Ruth Ann Thompson, *Designer*
Grace Hill, *Associate Managing Editor*
Michael O'Connor, *Production Editor*
Marfé Ferguson Delano, *Editor*
Paige Towler, *Editorial Assistant*
Erica Holsclaw, *Special Project Assistant*
Allie Allen and Sanjida Rashid,
    Design Production Assistants
Margaret Leist, *Photo Assistant*
Lewis R. Bassford, *Production Manager*
Susan Borke, *Legal and Business Affairs*

Production Services
Phillip L. Schlosser, *Senior Vice President*
Chris Brown, *Vice President,
    NG Book Manufacturing*
George Bounelis, *Senior Production Manager*
Nicole Elliott, *Director of Production*
Rachel Faulise, *Manager*
Robert L. Barr, *Manager*

For more information, please visit
www.nationalgeographic.com, call
1-800-NGS LINE (647-5463), or write
to the following address:

National Geographic Society
1145 17th Street N.W.
Washington, D.C. 20036-4688 U.S.A.

Visit us online at
www.nationalgeographic.com/books

For librarians and teachers:
www.ngchildrensbooks.org

National Geographic supports K–12
educators with ELA Common Core
Resources. Visit natgeoed.org/
commoncore for more information.

More for kids from National Geographic:
kids.nationalgeographic.com

For information about special discounts for
bulk purchases, please contact National
Geographic Books Special Sales:
ngspecsales@ngs.org

For rights or permissions inquiries, please
contact National Geographic Books Subsidiary
Rights: ngbookrights@ngs.org

Trade paperback
ISBN: 978-1-4263-1914-3
Reinforced library edition
ISBN: 978-1-4263-1916-7

Printed in China
14/RRDS/1

Table of CONTENTS

That's me, Brady Barr, with my friend Gerry Martin on the left. Together, we caught this giant Indian rock python.

The SNAKE That ATE COWS!

When catching a snake this big, it's always best to secure its head first. That's the biting end!

Chapter 1

SNAKE Problem!

I was waist-deep in water in a muddy swamp. I was trying not to think about the leeches that might be crawling up my legs. Then— I spotted it! Stretched out in front of me was the biggest snake I had ever seen. It looked as long as a bus!

What was I doing here? My name is Brady Barr. I'm a zoologist (sounds like zoh-AH-luh-gist), a scientist who studies animals. I've studied all kinds of animals all over the world. My favorites are reptiles—really big reptiles.

I've worked with some real giants. I've wrestled crocodiles over 18 feet (5.5 m) long. I've captured 10-foot (3-m)-long lizards and turtles the size of small cars.

But until that day in the swamp, I'd never come across a giant snake. Although they're among the biggest reptiles on the planet, they're very hard to find. And scientists know surprisingly little about them.

The swamp where I met the giant snake was in northern India. I was there with my friend Gerry Martin, a reptile expert. We had teamed up to study a rare and endangered crocodilian (sounds like krah-koh-DIL-ee-un). But our croc project soon took an unexpected turn.

Open Wide!

Some snakes can swallow things three times the size of their own head! How do they do it? Snakes have really flexible jaws. Human jaws are attached to the skull like a door on hinges. All we can do is open and shut them. A snake's lower jaw is not solidly attached at the chin, like ours is. Each side can move separately. A snake's jawbone is attached to the skull by stretchy bands of tissue, almost like rubber bands. Using its curved teeth to grip its prey, the snake can slowly stretch out its jaws and move its mouth around its meal.

When Gerry and I got to the small village near our research site, none of the people wanted to talk about crocs. All they wanted to talk about were snakes. They said they had a big problem. Their cows were disappearing. And they believed a giant snake was eating them.

Holy cow! I thought. *A cow-eating snake?*

This was a story we just *had* to look into. A snake large enough to eat a cow would have to be a true giant. We'd heard stories like this before. But no scientists had ever been able to check them out. Maybe this was our chance to prove those stories were true.

The villagers told us the giant snake

was eating their dogs, cats, and goats, too. They hoped maybe we could catch this snake and take it away to a safe place, far away from the village.

Gerry and I thought the snake was probably an Indian rock python. Rock pythons live in many different habitats. You can find them in low grasslands and on high mountain slopes. But the real giants usually stay near water.

The village was near the Geruwa (sounds like jeh-ROO-wah) River. Gerry wanted to go straight to the swampy area closest to the river, where the water was deepest. It was a great place for a big snake.

I really wanted to see this giant. But I wasn't so sure I wanted to get into a deep, muddy swamp with it!

Ten-year-old Ramkrishna helped Gerry and me find the huge snake.

Chapter 2

Swamp SLOG

Indian rock pythons can grow to more than 20 feet (6 m) long. They are incredibly strong. A python has more than 10,000 muscles (sounds like MUH-sels) in its body. Humans have fewer than 1,000. Pythons are constrictors (sounds like kun-STRICT-ers). That means they use their muscles to squeeze, or constrict, their prey.

When a python sees an animal

it wants to eat, it strikes out with lightning speed. It latches on to it with needle-sharp teeth. The teeth curve backward, toward the snake's throat. Once an animal is caught in those teeth, it cannot pull away. The snake instantly coils around it and squeezes. When the prey has died, the python opens its mouth wide and swallows it whole.

A snake big enough to swallow a cow could certainly swallow a man! With this thought in my head, I waded into the dark water. I had never seen a truly giant snake in the wild before. But I knew it would be better to find it before it found me. I did not want to experience a python's big squeeze.

Gerry and I searched for a long time without seeing anything. Then we decided it might be better if we split up. That way we could search more ground—or swamp, that is. Pretty soon, I heard Gerry shouting, "Snake! Snake! Snake!" I nearly jumped out of my skin.

I slogged toward Gerry through the knee-deep water. Peering through the tall grass, I could see he had a small, three-foot (1-m)-long python in his grasp. This was very cool. But I was expecting something a little larger. This couldn't be the cow-eater, that's for sure. We split up again and kept searching. After several hours, all we'd found were three more small pythons.

Exhausted, we sat on the riverbank and picked the leeches off our bare legs. After all our effort, we had found only four small snakes. We felt frustrated.

Super Smellers

A snake smells with its nose, like humans do. But a snake has another secret weapon in the world of smell—its forked tongue. A snake flicks its tongue in the air. The two tips pick up tiny particles of odor. When the snake pulls its tongue in, the odor particles are delivered to a special organ on the roof of its mouth, called the Jacobson's organ. This helps the snake identify the odors. Together, the nose and Jacobson's organ make the snake a super smeller!

We wanted to get back to the croc study we'd come to India for in the first place. We were both thinking this giant snake story was simply that: a tall tale! We had about decided to call it quits, when a small boy, about ten years old, came up to us. His name was Ramkrishna (sounds like ram-KRISH-nah). He had been watching us all day. He said that he really liked snakes. And he told us we were looking for the snake in the wrong spot.

Ramkrishna said the big snake liked to hang out in another part of the swamp, in an area farther from the river. Gerry wasn't so sure. He still felt we'd find the snake closer to the river. He said he was going to take one more look.

I decided to check out the area Ramkrishna told us about. So, Gerry and I separated again for one last slog through the muck. We agreed to meet up at our truck before sunset.

By now, I was pretty sure there was no giant cow-eating snake. I was feeling a lot more relaxed in the swamp. But I was not crazy about the leeches! I was trudging along, wondering if any of those slimy little things were crawling on me again. I reached down to scratch my leg. And when I looked up, there it was! I froze in disbelief. I was horrified and fascinated at the same time. Never in my life had I seen a snake so big!

Ramkrishna had been right. Farther from the river, the snake had found a nice spot to come out of the water. Here it could warm up in the sunshine. But it could slide back into the water quickly, if it needed to.

At first, I thought maybe the snake was asleep in the warm sun. But there's no way to know for sure if a snake is asleep. Snakes don't have eyelids, so their eyes are always open.

I watched for any little movement. Suddenly, I saw the snake's long forked tongue flick out. It waved around in the air in long, drawn-out motions.

Uh oh! I thought. *It knows I'm here!* Snakes use their forked tongues to pick up odors. And right now that giant was smelling me.

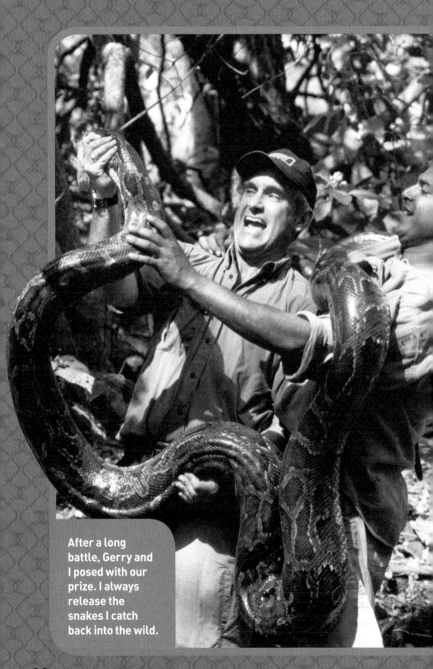

After a long battle, Gerry and I posed with our prize. I always release the snakes I catch back into the wild.

Chapter 3

Wrestling a GIANT

My brain began racing with scary thoughts. I was only a few feet away from an animal that could swallow me whole. If it decided to strike, I wouldn't be able to move away fast enough.

"Snake! Giant snake! Giant snake!" I yelled. I was startled by the sound of my own voice in the silent swamp.

I knew my screams wouldn't startle the snake, because snakes don't have ears like we do. But I sure hoped Gerry was close enough to hear me.

With my eyes still glued to the snake, I heard Gerry slogging toward me. When he spotted the giant python, his eyes grew as big as plates.

Gerry had more experience with big snakes than I had. But he had never seen one this large. "We have to catch it!" he shouted.

"Catch it?" I cried. "Are you kidding me? That thing could eat us both for lunch." I had a better idea: *Let's not catch it. Let's run for our lives.* But I kept that thought to myself. I knew Gerry was right. We had to try and capture this snake

before it got into any more trouble.
If it did, the villagers might harm it.

"On the count of three, jump on it,"
Gerry said. "I'll go for the head.
You secure the body."

Secure the body? I thought. *That snake looks a lot stronger than I am.* Still, that sounded easier than trying to grab the toothy end. There's nothing fancy about catching a big snake. Just jump on top of it and hang on. And avoid the mouth. It's just a matter of muscle against muscle. Or in this case, our combined total of less than 2,000 muscles against the snake's 10,000!

"One, two ..." Gerry counted.

Three came way too quickly! I saw Gerry launch himself toward the big snake. I followed at about the count of three and a half. I wanted to make sure he had the head and all those teeth under control before I tackled the writhing (sounds like RYE-thing) body.

As soon as my hands touched that snake, I knew we were in big trouble. Instantly, it began to wrap us both up in its coils. It started throwing us around in the muddy water. Ramkrishna had been watching us from a safe distance. Now he ran to find his older brother to help us.

Gerry and I held on for dear life. Everything was a blur of coils, teeth, and scales. Suddenly the snake threw a coil around my neck! Within seconds, I could barely breathe. I became light-headed, and I was close to passing out. The battle seemed to go on forever.

The Big Squeeze

Rock pythons and other constrictors don't just coil around something and squeeze. It's more complicated than that. Each time a constrictor's struggling prey breathes out, the snake tightens its coils. With each squeeze, the prey has a harder time taking a breath. Eventually, the coils become so tight, blood can no longer move around the prey's body. Studies have shown that a snake can feel the heartbeat of its prey. Only when it senses the heart stop does the snake release its strong hold. In this picture, the snake is preying on a lizard.

But then, almost without warning, the snake loosened its grip on my neck. The huge reptile had tired itself out.

We were going to be okay. And we had captured the giant! As we struggled to drag it out of the swamp, we guessed that it was about 16 feet (5 m) long. It felt like it weighed more than both of us put together.

With the help of Ramkrishna and his big brother, we hoisted the giant Indian rock python on our shoulders. We couldn't wait to show off our prize. The villagers would be so happy. The news of the big snake spread fast. We soon found ourselves surrounded by a crowd. Everyone stared at the snake. But no one said a word.

Finally I broke the silence. "Here it is!" I cried. "Here's the giant snake that's been

eating your cows!"
I expected everyone to
cheer. But there was
only silence. The people exchanged
puzzled glances. After what seemed like
a long time, one man finally spoke up.
"This isn't the giant cow-eating snake,"
he said. "This isn't even a big one."

"Not even a big one?" I said. "You have
got to be kidding me!"

Gerry and I stared at each other in
disbelief. Without saying a word, we knew
we were both thinking the same thing.
*If this is a small one, we don't want any
part of a big one!* We were battered,
bruised, and beat up. The villagers just
smiled, as they watched us carry our
snake back toward the swamp.

ROBO-WEASEL

The cover created for my remote-controlled robot looked like a weasel to me, so I named the robot "Robo-Weasel."

This is me, crawling into an aardvark burrow, or hole. It was deep, dark, and dangerous in there. And smelly, too!

Chapter 1

Not Going in There!

Catching snakes can be dangerous work. Often the hardest part of the job is just finding the snake you're looking for. Snakes are good at hiding. The colors and patterns on their skin help them blend in with their surroundings.

The best way to find snakes is to look in places where they like to hang out. When it gets hot, snakes look for cool nooks and crannies to get into. Some of their favorite places are hollow logs, caves, cracks in rock walls, and burrows.

After my trip to India, I was excited about finding more giant snakes. I soon got the chance to help a group of reptile experts in South Africa. They were hoping to find out more about the African rock python. And I was hoping to weigh and measure them for research.

African rock pythons are one of the largest snakes on Earth. They can grow more than 16 feet (5 m) long. They spend a lot of time underground in burrows. The snakes can't dig holes on their own, so they use burrows made by other animals. One of the rock python's favorites is the aardvark (sounds like ARD-vark) burrow.

Cold-Blooded

Lots of people call snakes and other reptiles "cold-blooded." But their blood isn't really cold. A better word to describe cold-blooded animals is "ectothermic" (sounds like EK-toe-THERM-ick). "Ecto" means "outside," and "therm" means "heat." So, being an ectotherm means getting warmth from outside sources. When ectotherms are cold, they warm themselves up in the sun. When they get too hot, they go into water or into the shade.

An aardvark looks a lot like a pig except it has goofy rabbit ears and a long snout. Its burrows are big enough for a person to crawl into. At least they are for someone who's crazy enough to try it.

You never know who might be inside the burrow. An average aardvark weighs about 150 pounds (68 kg). Its hooflike claws are strong enough to tear apart big termite mounds. So, an angry aardvark would be bad enough. But there could be a hyena, or even a leopard in there!

Sometimes venomous (sounds like VEN-uh-muss) snakes call the burrows home. A few years ago, I crawled down a burrow and came face-to-face with a cobra. It was *not* happy to see me! It lunged at me, trying to bite me again and again. A cobra's venom can kill a grown man in minutes. That was one of the closest calls I have ever had with any animal. After that, I promised myself I'd never crawl down a burrow again.

But I needed to weigh and measure pythons for my research. And aardvark burrows are the best places to find them. Day after day I searched the savanna—the dry, open grasslands where African rock pythons live. I did not see any. It was so frustrating. Maybe dozens of them were hiding underground. But I was too scared to crawl into a burrow to find out. And the time had come for me to head home.

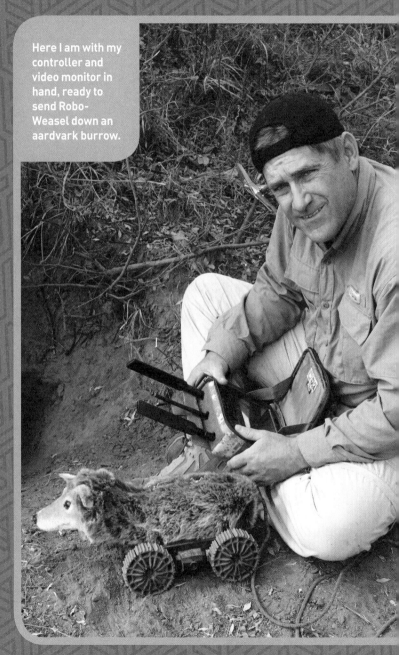

Here I am with my controller and video monitor in hand, ready to send Robo-Weasel down an aardvark burrow.

Chapter 2

FISHING for Snakes

A few months later, I saw an interesting news report on television. It was all about firefighters and police using robots to do their most dangerous work. This gave me a great idea that might just solve my problem. Crawling down an aardvark's burrow is definitely dangerous work. If a robot could crawl into a burning building for a firefighter, it could crawl down a burrow for me. It was brilliant! Now I just had to find a robot.

I found out I needed to talk to a roboticist (sounds like row-BAHT-uh-sist). That's someone who designs, builds, and programs robots. I went to visit one. He showed me a small remote-controlled robot with a built-in camera. I pictured myself driving this thing down dangerous burrows. And I would get to stay safe and sound aboveground!

It seemed like a great plan. But I thought of one small problem. The robot was only the size of a shoe box. It could locate the snake. But even if we gave it a strong robotic arm, it wouldn't be big enough to catch a giant python. I would still have to crawl down the burrow to get the snake out.

Unlike cobras, pythons are not venomous. But they can be very bad-tempered. After my brush with the cobra, I didn't want to be stuck in a burrow with an angry snake of any kind.

Then I had a crazy idea. My robot couldn't catch a python, but maybe a python could catch my robot! What if I made the robot look like something the snake would want to eat? If it thought the robot was a small animal, it might grab it and wrap it in its powerful coils. Then all I would have to do is pull the robot out of the burrow by its safety rope—with the big snake attached! It would be like fishing for snakes.

Did You Know?

Snakes can't crawl backward. They can move forward in lots of different ways, but they can never back up.

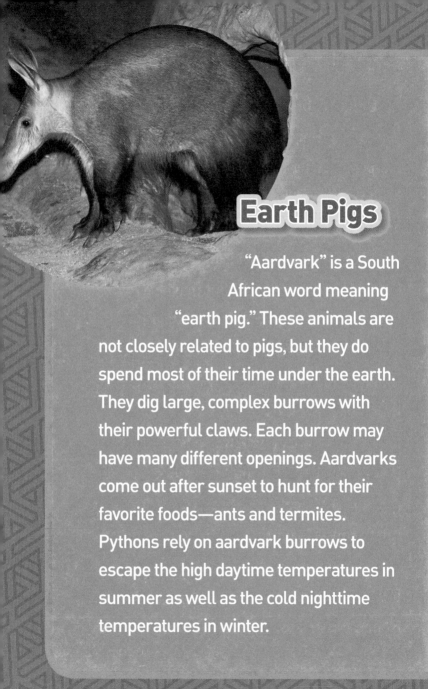

Earth Pigs

"Aardvark" is a South African word meaning "earth pig." These animals are not closely related to pigs, but they do spend most of their time under the earth. They dig large, complex burrows with their powerful claws. Each burrow may have many different openings. Aardvarks come out after sunset to hunt for their favorite foods—ants and termites. Pythons rely on aardvark burrows to escape the high daytime temperatures in summer as well as the cold nighttime temperatures in winter.

I took my new robot to my friend Paul Rhymer. He works at a museum as an animal modeler. It's his job to make all the animals on display look as lifelike as possible. Paul made me an awesome animal disguise to fit over my robot. He told me he made it look like a black-backed jackal. That's a foxlike animal pythons love to eat. I thought it looked more like a weasel. So I decided to name it Robo-Weasel.

A few weeks later, I was back in South Africa. I stood over my first aardvark burrow with Robo-Weasel under one arm. I couldn't wait to try this. I set the robot on the ground next to the burrow's entrance. Then I set up the video monitor. That would let me see everything Robo-Weasel's camera was seeing. I grabbed the controller and sent the robot down the hole.

It was so nice to be looking at the inside of an aardvark burrow without having to be down in that gloom myself. Everything was working perfectly. But I wasn't finding anything. I didn't see so much as a cricket! I sent Robo-Weasel to the very end of the burrow. No one was home. I pulled the robot back to the surface. Then I headed off in search of another burrow.

It wasn't long before I found one. I sent the robot down again. But there was nothing in this burrow, either. I tried a third burrow, and then a fourth, and even a fifth. All I found for all that effort was one ugly spider. Robo-Weasel was working great. But where were all the snakes? I started thinking maybe they had all moved to a new neighborhood!

Then I found a sixth burrow. This time I gave Robo-Weasel a pat on the head for good luck. I sent him down. I watched as the robot went deeper and deeper. The tunnel made a slight turn up ahead. I moved the robot carefully around it. And that's when I saw it. Right in front of the camera was a big snake!

I was so excited. I stared at the video screen. Was it a rock python? It looked kind of brown and dusty. Then I realized it wasn't a snake at all. It was a tree root. I had been fooled.

With help from Robo-Weasel and my cameraman, I finally managed to nab this huge African rock python.

Chapter 3

RESCUING Robo-Weasel!

With hope fading fast, I drove Robo-Weasel even deeper into the tunnel. Soon it was in a large chamber. *This is where the aardvark must sleep,* I thought. *It's an aardvark bedroom.* The robot had stirred up a lot of dust. I stopped and waited for the dust to settle, so I could get a better view of the chamber. Then *BAM!* It happened!

On the video screen I saw a giant python's head rocket out of the dusty darkness straight at the robot's camera. It scared me so much, I fell over backward and knocked the monitor over.

I hurried to get it set up again. All I could see now were giant squeezing coils. My plan had worked! The python had grabbed Robo-Weasel and was now putting on the big squeeze. Finally I had caught my snake. Now all I had to do was reel it in.

I grabbed the rope and started tugging. I pulled, I heaved, I hauled. But nothing happened. It was like my robot was tied to an anchor. I got a better grip on the rope. I planted my feet on either side of the burrow and pulled with all my might. Still the robot wouldn't budge.

All this time, my friend Eric Cochran had been filming me for a National Geographic TV show. I gave him a desperate look. He set his camera down and began pulling, too. We pulled so hard, I was afraid the rope was going to break.

I knew there was only one solution. I was going to have to do something I had promised myself I'd never do again. If I was ever going to see my Robo-Weasel again, I was going to have to crawl down that burrow. I felt sick to my stomach. But if I was going to do this, I had to do it soon. I wanted to get to the snake before it realized the weasel wasn't a real meal. Otherwise I might end up as its next choice!

I got on my belly and slid down the dusty tunnel. It smelled bad. And it was a tight fit, with no room to turn around. I wormed my way down as fast as I could. I knew the giant python must be just up ahead. Thoughts of its needle-sharp teeth and powerful coils raced through my mind. *Maybe I should just let the snake keep the robot,* I thought.

Then I spotted it. It was still wrapped around the robot. It looked a lot bigger in person than it did on the video monitor.

I lunged forward and grabbed it. This snake was solid, powerful muscle! I searched for the head. When catching any snake, the first thing you need to do is secure the head—the biting end! I could see the snake's head tucked under its own coils. It still had the weasel in its jaws.

Out of Its Skin

Have you ever come across a dry, empty snake skin outdoors? Often it's the first clue that there are snakes in the area. Snakes shed their skin when they outgrow it. The skin usually begins to come loose around the snake's nose first. Then the snake slowly works its way out of its old skin. It pulls off in one big piece, inside out. It's a little like when you pull a shirt off over your head. A snake will shed its skin several times during its lifetime.

Using both hands, I turned the snake, so it would slide out of the tunnel more easily. Then I tried inching out backward. With the whole coiled mass of snake and robot in my hands, it was impossible. I couldn't turn around. And I was not going to let go of the snake now that I'd caught it!

It would be only a matter of seconds before the snake let go of the weasel. Then I would be in real trouble. Eric was my only hope.

"Come down the burrow and grab me by the ankles," I shouted. "You're going to have to pull me out!"

A few moments later, I felt Eric's hands on my ankles. He pulled me up the tunnel. I held on tight to my prize.

We popped out of the burrow into the sunlight. The python dropped the weasel. I knew I had only one chance to grab the snake before it grabbed me. I lunged and caught it right behind the head.

The big python was exhausted from squeezing. I was exhausted. Eric was exhausted. Robo-Weasel was probably exhausted, too. Eric and I lay in the dirt, trying to catch our breath. Too bad there was no one to film us!

"You know what," I said, "next time I'll bring two robots. One to crawl down the burrow and find the snake. And one to crawl down and save the first robot!"

Helped by a group of local people, my friend Mark Auliya (third from left) and I show off the reticulated python we caught.

SNAKE
on a
STRING

I spotted this reticulated python slithering off the riverbank into the water. Pythons are great swimmers.

Chapter 1

The Snake PALACE

Years ago, I heard about a mysterious cave on a small island in Indonesia (sounds like IN-doh-NEE-zhuh). The local people call it the Snake Palace. They say that hundreds of snakes live in that cave. And not just any snakes! This cave is home to the longest snake on the planet—the reticulated (sounds like reh-TICK-you-lay-ted) python.

I wanted to see those snakes for myself. So I got excited when my friend Mark Auliya (sounds like eye-OOL-ee-ah), a python expert, told me about his new project. He was going to research big snakes living in caves. The Snake Palace seemed like the perfect place to start. I teamed up with Mark, and we headed for Indonesia.

We flew to a landing strip on a remote island. From there it took us three days to get to the village closest to the cave. A few of the people there offered to lead us to the cave. They took us up and down two mountains. Then I started smelling something really bad. Our guides said the cave was also home to thousands of bats. Bats had lived there for hundreds of years. The horrible smell was from the bat poop!

Finally, I spotted the cave entrance. It didn't look like a palace. It looked like a muddy hole in the rock wall. One of our guides suddenly grabbed my shoulder. He pointed to a bush near the entrance. An angry-looking tree viper stared back at me. We counted six of these deadly snakes in the bushes. Our guides said the vipers are always there, waiting to strike at bats as they fly in and out of the cave.

Our guides warned us that the cave was full of danger. We might meet cobras, scorpions, and giant centipedes. If we survived those, we still had to face all that bat poop, quicksand, and poisonous gases. Mark and I shrugged. We'd come too far to turn back now. We waded in.

The nasty smell made my eyes water. It was all I could do not to vomit. Moving deeper into the cave, I began to hear the high-pitched squeaking of the bats. It sounded like millions of them. We tried to stay close to the cave wall, because that's where the bat poop was less deep. It was already up to our knees.

The farther we went, the more bats we saw. They flapped around our faces. And now the bat poop was waist-deep. It was like wading through a thick soup. The bats were really starting to freak me out, when I saw it: my first reticulated python.

Komodo dragon

leatherback sea turtle

Land of Giants

The country of Indonesia could be called the land of giants— giant reptiles, that is! It is home to the world's longest snake, the reticulated python, and the world's largest venomous snake, the king cobra. Indonesia is also home to the Komodo dragon, the largest lizard on Earth, and the saltwater crocodile, the largest croc on the planet. The world's biggest turtle is also found in Indonesia. It's called the leatherback sea turtle.

saltwater crocodile

The snake was resting on a small rock ledge. It looked about six feet (2 m) long. I reached out to grab it, when Mark yelled, "Snake!" He had spotted one, too. Suddenly the poop smell and the bats didn't seem so bad. We were finding pythons!

Mark and I caught and measured many pythons. The deeper we went into the cave, the bigger the snakes seemed to get. Then I saw a large crack in the cave wall up ahead. I decided to squeeze in and take a look around. Just in front of me, I spotted gigantic coils. Those coils looked bigger around than I am. This looked like a world-record snake.

The only way to know for sure would be to get the snake out and measure it. We decided to tickle and prod the snake with my snake tongs. Maybe that would make it come out. Once it did, we were ready to jump on it and hold on for dear life!

I tickled the big snake. It shifted its coils a little. Mark prodded the snake. Nothing.

After an hour, it was clear to us that the snake wasn't going anywhere. Disappointed, we left the giant snake in the crack and went on with our work. That night we talked about the big snake and decided we'd try again tomorrow.

Early the next morning, we went straight back to the crack. But the big snake was gone! Except for a few bats, the crack was empty. We measured lots of pythons over the next few days. But the time came to head home, and we had not seen the giant snake again.

We found reticulated pythons of many sizes in the cave. This small one was resting on some tree roots.

Chapter 2

A Brilliant PLAN

When I got back to the United States, I told all my friends about the giant snake in the crack. "It's a world-record snake!" I said. I don't think they believed me.

I knew Mark was planning on going back to the cave several times over the next year. I decided to go with him. I couldn't stop thinking about that big snake.

Finally, the time came to return to Indonesia and the Snake Palace. Mark and I were so excited, we almost ran through the cave to the crack. When we got there, I dived right into the hole.

The big snake was there! It was in exactly the same place as the last time! I tried to urge it out of the crack with my snake tongs. But again, the big snake hardly moved a muscle.

I let Mark try. Again, nothing.

We couldn't think of any other way to get that snake out. Just like last time, we went on to catch many snakes in the cave. None of them were giants like the one in the crack. The next day, we went back. And, just like before, the snake was gone. We never saw it again on that trip, either.

It's the Pits!

Pythons can see with their eyes, just like we humans can. But they have another tool that allows them to see in total darkness. Along their lips are small holes, or pits. These pit organs can sense very, very small differences in temperature. This allows the python to detect, or spot, a warm bat inside a cool, dark cave. Having these built-in heat detectors gives the snake a big advantage over its prey.

This is how a python "sees," or senses, your hand. Red and yellow show the warmer areas, and blues and greens show the cooler parts.

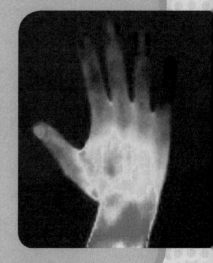

When we got home, of course everyone asked us about the giant snake. I told them we'd seen it again. "He's bigger around than my whole body!" I said. This time when I told the story, people shook their heads. They thought I was making the whole thing up. I knew I had to go back to the cave and somehow catch that snake.

While I waited for our next trip, I talked to my daughter, Isabella. She said she had an idea of how to catch the snake. She drew me a picture. Her drawing showed a big snake attached to a giant ball of string. She explained that all I had to do was attach the end of the string to the snake. Then tickle the snake, just like before. When the snake decided to leave the crack, it would have the string attached to it. All I'd have to do was follow the string, and I would find the snake. It was just that easy.

I thought about Isabella's plan. At first it seemed silly to try to catch a giant snake with a ball of string. But the more I thought about it, the more brilliant her plan seemed. I got myself a ball of string and packed it with my gear. This would be our last trip to the Snake Palace, so I was nervous. If we weren't able to catch the big snake this time, no one would ever believe us.

Did You Know?

The world's largest ball of string is in Cawker City, Kansas. It weighs more than 19,000 pounds (8,618 kg) and stands over eight feet (2.5 m) tall.

Capturing and measuring pythons in this cave meant getting covered from head to toe in stinky bat poop every single day!

Chapter 3

FOLLOW That String!

Before we headed for the cave, Mark and I had to figure out how we were going to attach the string to the snake. It's not easy to attach anything to a snake! We decided to use a sticky bandage strip. We'd poke a hole in the strip, thread the string through the hole, and then tie the end of the string to a toothpick so it wouldn't pull out.

All we had to do was stick the bandage strip onto the snake.

When we got to the cave, we jumped right into the bat-poop soup and went straight to the crack. I took off my backpack and wedged myself into the hole. There it was! The python's giant coils were right in front of me. I gripped the bandage and string with my snake tongs. I reached way in and put the bandage on the snake. I pressed it with my tongs, to make sure it stuck. Then we left the big ball of string on the cave floor.

We captured and measured a lot of snakes that day. But it was hard to concentrate. Our minds were on the big snake and the ball of string. That night, back at our camp, we talked for hours about the snake. I don't think we slept a wink.

Before the sun came up the next morning, Mark and I headed back to the cave. When we got to the entrance, Mark shouted, "Look! The string!" The snake had left the cave, and it was trailing our string behind it.

We followed the string. We went under branches, over rocks, through bushes, and down toward the river. Then the string disappeared into a spooky-looking bamboo forest. We followed it through the bamboo and along a rocky wall. We came to a sharp turn. Around the corner, there was the snake! It looked even bigger than I had imagined.

The New Cute and Cuddly

Many types of pythons are in big trouble in the wild. Their numbers are decreasing, because humans are killing them. Sometimes people kill snakes simply because they don't like them. Sometimes snakes are hunted for their skins, which are made into shoes, handbags, and belts.

Snakes aren't cute and cuddly, at least not to most people. But pythons are just as important to their ecosystems as the cute and cuddly animals of the world. So spread the word: Snake skins belong on pythons, not handbags!

"Wow," Mark said. "We're definitely going to need some help."

I knew he was right. This snake was way too big for just two people to handle. It could easily kill us both in its powerful coils. We ducked behind the rocky wall, where the snake couldn't see us. Mark said he'd run to the village to get help.

I was uneasy all by myself with the giant snake. What if it decided to cross the river? What if it went into another cave or back to the Snake Palace? What if we lost it?

Luckily, only minutes later, I heard Mark yelling for me. He burst through the bamboo forest with a bunch of people behind him. They had been on their way to the river to go fishing. Mark told them about our giant snake, and they were all happy to help. What luck!

Now there were 12 of us to hold the big python. But the snake was starting to move. We had to act fast! We ran out from behind the rocky wall. When we closed in on the snake, it got angry and started striking at us. Yikes! I wasn't sure I wanted to jump on this snake, especially the toothy end. But the others couldn't get too close, until I secured the head. Man, its head was about the size of a large dog's.

I took a deep breath and launched myself toward it. My hands could barely fit around its neck, but I held on with all my might. The snake started throwing me around with its powerful muscles. The rest of the guys jumped on its back. The giant python tossed all 12 of us around as it struggled. Finally I could feel it was getting tired. The snake stopped thrashing.

We had done it! Isabella's plan had worked. We measured the snake. It was a whopping 21 feet (6.5 m) long. It was the longest snake I have ever captured. It wasn't a world record, but after feeling the power of that python, I'm pretty sure everyone was happy it wasn't any bigger.

After taking some pictures, we let the snake go. It went straight to the river and swam away. I looked around at everyone. Big smiles lit up every face. I was all smiles, too. Now I knew everyone back home would believe my big snake story. I had the pictures to prove it!

While I handle the toothy end, scientist Maria Muñoz holds the tail end of a giant green anaconda.

SOCK
HEAD

Green anacondas can strike and bite very quickly! That's why I'm holding this one firmly near the head.

Chapter 1

BIGGEST of the BIG

The reticulated python may be the longest snake in the world. But there is one snake that can grow even heavier and bigger around. It's the green anaconda (sounds like AN-uh-CON-duh). These snakes can weigh more than 250 pounds (113 kg). A few giants have been found that weighed over 500 pounds (227 kg)!

This is a snake I have always

wanted to see. My friend Maria Muñoz (sounds like MOON-yoz) studies anacondas in South America. She has found hundreds of these snakes. If anyone could help me get up close to a giant anaconda, it would be Maria.

I called her to see if I could help with her research. Scientists still know very little about anacondas. That's because they stay out of sight. They spend most of their lives underwater.

Maria told me to come on down and meet her at her field site in Venezuela (sounds like VEN-is-ZWALE-uh). It was in the region of grassy plains called the Llanos (sounds like YAH-nose).

Anacondas love the Llanos. The plains get flooded during the rainy season each

Did You Know?

Anacondas sometimes eat other anacondas. They are snake cannibals!

year. The water helps support the snakes' weight and makes it easier for them to move around. When you are a 200-pound (91-kg) snake, it's a lot easier to float and swim than it is to crawl.

An anaconda's nostrils and eyes are on top of its head. This lets it stay almost completely hidden underwater. With just the top of its head peeking out, it can see and smell its prey. But its prey can't see it. That's great for the anaconda's hunting success. But it sure makes it hard for us to find it!

An anaconda has over 100 needle-sharp teeth. It even has two rows of teeth on the roof of its mouth. But these teeth are not made for chewing. They curve backward, toward the snake's throat.

Once hooked by those teeth, even a large animal cannot pull free. The snake soon wraps its prey in its coils. Like pythons, anacondas are constrictors. They squeeze their prey to death.

A large anaconda is powerful enough to kill the small crocs that also live in the Llanos. But its favorite prey is the capybara (sounds like cap-ee-BAR-uh). The capybara is the world's largest rodent. A capybara can be the size of a large dog. Many of them here weigh well over 100 pounds (45 kg).

So, in the Llanos we have the world's largest snake hunting the world's largest rodent. It made sense to me. I just hoped I wasn't going to be the world's largest chicken when it came time to jump on a big anaconda!

Truth or Fiction?

As far back as the 1500s, early explorers of South America reported anacondas of monstrous size. Some claimed they'd seen snakes more than 100 feet (30 m) long! Were these measurements accurate? Or were they the products of wild imaginations? We'll never know. What we do know is that giant snakes are hard to measure. Even today, scientists have a hard time getting exact measurements. We can only wonder if those old reports of 100-foot (30-m) snakes were based on fact or fantasy.

This anaconda was about as long as I am tall, but I was hoping to find an even bigger one!

Chapter 2

FIND THEM With Your FEET!

When I got to the field site, Maria explained how she and the other scientists on her team find the anacondas. You have to get in the murky waters on the Llanos and feel around for them with your feet. You just have to make sure you find the snake before it finds you. An anaconda strike is lightning fast!

Maria said it was best to wade in barefoot. I imagined the dark water full of snakes. I imagined all those snakes eager to bite my bare feet. I decided to keep my shoes on.

Maria and I walked slowly through the knee-deep water. We felt around with our feet. I was pretty nervous at first. But hours and hours went by, and we didn't find so much as a frog. Then, suddenly I heard Maria scream, "Snake!"

She was pretty far away from me. I ran toward her, as fast as I could through the water. I expected to see her wrestling a giant snake. Instead she was holding a cute little snake, no more than a foot (30 cm) long. It was a baby anaconda. Maria said they are even more difficult to find than the big ones. I was happy to finally get to see an anaconda. But it wasn't quite what I'd expected.

Unlike pythons, female anacondas don't lay eggs. They give birth to live babies. The females here in the Llanos will have 20 to 40 babies at one time. So there could be other anaconda babies close by.

We let the baby go and continued our search for a giant. We were hopeful. If there are babies, there are probably adults around, too! This little guy had to have parents. And we were determined to find them.

We hadn't gone far when once again I heard Maria yelling, "Snake!"

This time it was different. I could already see she was struggling with a huge one. And it did not look happy.

How Far Can a Snake Strike?

WARNING, THERE'S MATH INVOLVED!

A snake can strike as far as one-third of its body length. So, whenever I'm trying to catch one, I estimate its length. Say the anaconda I've found is 18 feet (5.5 m) long. How far can it strike out? Can you do the math in your head? Eighteen divided by three equals ... I quickly calculate that the strike zone is six feet (1.8 m). Anything closer, and I would be in the danger zone. Now that's a good reason to study hard and practice your math!

"Brady, get over here and grab the head!" she shouted.

Yikes, I thought. *The head … the toothy biting end.* Determined not to let the snake get away, I searched for its head. With snake coils moving in all directions, the water was already churned into a muddy froth. I could hardly see a thing. It was chaos (sounds like KAY-oss)!

Then, the snake came up for a breath of air. I spotted its head right away, and I leaped toward it. I grabbed the snake behind the head with both hands. Whoa, I could not believe how strong the snake was! And it was so thick, my hands didn't even reach around it.

Maria and I stumbled and struggled with the snake. But we finally got it out of the water. These snakes are powerful, but they tire out quickly, if you can just hang on.

Maria, the snake, and I lay on the muddy ground. We were all exhausted. But we humans didn't have much time to rest. Maria said it was time to gather some scientific data. I sat on top of the snake and held it down so Maria could measure it. It was about 12 feet (3.5 m) long, and it weighed 70 pounds (32 kg).

Maria explained that after she measured and weighed each snake, she clipped a few of its scales. This didn't hurt the snake, but it would help her tell when she caught the same snake again.

While Maria was recording her data, I looked out toward the horizon. I saw something shining in the sun far away. It looked like a really big crocodile had just crawled out of the water. *Yikes,* I thought, *Maria didn't tell me there were big crocs around here.* I looked back down at the snake and tried to focus on helping Maria.

Then it hit me like a bolt of lightning! That wasn't a big crocodile. Crocs that size don't live here. It had to be a monstrously big snake.

I jumped up and started running toward it. Without even thinking, I left Maria all alone with the snake she was trying to measure.

I ran as fast as I could, screaming, "Snake! Snake! Snake!"

This green anaconda was the biggest snake I have ever helped to capture! Can you guess what that is over its head?

Chapter 3

PHOTO OP!

Boy, was this snake huge! As I got closer, I could tell the anaconda was at least twice the size of the one we had just caught. I looked over my shoulder. Maria had let the first snake go, and she was running to catch up with me.

Up close, the snake was truly terrifying. I took a deep breath and tried to ignore my fear. I tackled it near the head and held on for dear life. Maria quickly got a good grip on it, too. The giant snake threw us around with its massive coils.

"We just caught a monster!" I screamed. Maria and I both hung on tight. We could feel the anaconda slowly beginning to tire itself out.

"This could be the biggest snake I've ever caught!" cried Maria.

As soon as the snake had calmed down a little, it was time to find out. As I held the snake, Maria ran a tape measure along its back. It's not easy to measure a wriggling, writhing snake, so scientists usually measure them three times. You almost always get three different measurements!

Maria measured our monster three times and took an average. The anaconda turned out to be just over 17 feet (5 m) long. Boy oh boy, that is a whopper in my book. But Maria has captured some that were over 19 feet (6 m).

Anacondas are the heaviest snakes on the planet. I couldn't wait to find out how much this big girl weighed. Maria was sure the snake was a female. Female anacondas are always much larger than the males.

We had to call three of Maria's assistants to come help us. We planned to get the big snake into a bag. Then we would hang the bag from a scale, which we had attached to a nearby tree limb. As we wrestled the snake into the bag, I imagined that limb snapping under the weight.

Even with four of us lifting, we could barely move the snake. Finally, we hoisted it up and hooked the bag to the scale. I held my breath as the needle on the scale bobbed up and down. When it came to rest, we were all astonished.

It weighed 227 pounds (103 kg). "We've caught over 800 anacondas for this project, and this is the heaviest one yet," Maria said.

I knew that Maria would show me an anaconda. But this was bigger than anything in my wildest dreams. A supersize anaconda! What a great day! I definitely wanted my photo taken with this giant.

Snake Reward!

The New York Zoological (sounds like zoh-uh-LOJ-eh-cul) Society was one of America's first conservation organizations. Starting in the early 1900s, they offered a reward for anyone who could find a 30-foot (9-m)-long snake and bring it, alive and in good health, to the Bronx Zoo. Years passed, and the reward got larger and larger. It got up to $50,000. Still, no one ever brought the zoo a snake of this size. The reward was discontinued in 2002. The society decided it wasn't such a great idea to encourage people to disturb giant, dangerous snakes.

Maria grabbed the camera. But it was hard to get all of me and all of the snake in the same photo. Maria said, "Try lying down next to the snake."

I had a big smile on my face as I lay down next to it. But the snake was not as happy as I was. It opened its mouth wide and lunged at me. Yikes! It lunged again and again, as fast as lightning. I did my best to dodge its bites. All the while I was yelling to Maria, "Take it, take it! Take the picture!"

Maria started laughing. It was clear this just wasn't going to work.

I wanted a picture more than anything. But that giant anaconda would not stay still. I knew I needed something to calm the snake down and to hold its mouth shut so it couldn't bite me.

Then I realized I had just the thing.

I started to untie one of my shoes. Maria looked puzzled. "Don't worry," I told her. "I have an idea."

Off came my shoe, and then one of my wet, smelly old socks. Quickly and carefully, I pulled the sock over the anaconda's big head. Now it couldn't see me and it couldn't bite me. But I bet that snake didn't like the smell of my dirty old sock. *Pee-yew!*

I lay down next to the snake, and Maria snapped my photo. Then we pulled the sock off the snake's head and let it go.

I sure was happy. I think the snake looked happy, too. But I'm not sure if it was happy to be free, or just happy to get away from my smelly old sock!

THE END

DON'T MISS!

National Geographic Kids CHAPTERS

PARROT GENIUS!

And More True Stories of **Amazing Animal Talents**

By Moira Rose Donohue

Turn the page for a sneak preview . . .

Einstein joined the Knoxville Zoo in Tennessee when she was five years old.

Chapter 1

IT'S A ZOO HERE!

Imagine you're at the zoo. You hear a tiger growl. That's not surprising. Lots of zoos have tigers. But what if you're nowhere near the tiger exhibit? Next you hear a chimp screech. But there are no chimps around. And then a pirate says, *"Arrgh!"* Is it some kind of trick? Not if you're at the Knoxville (sounds like NOX-vil) Zoo in Knoxville, Tennessee, U.S.A.

It means you've just found Einstein, one of the most amazing parrots in the world!

Einstein joined the Knoxville Zoo more than 20 years ago. The zoo wanted to put together an animal show. It hired an animal talent scout. That's someone who looks for awesome animals that can learn to perform. When the talent scout heard about a very smart five-year-old parrot named Einstein, he knew he had to meet her.

Einstein is an African gray parrot. In the wild, African grays live in large groups called flocks. Some flocks have 100 birds. Living in such large groups makes them social, or friendly, with each other.

African gray parrots live in the rain

forests of Africa. But Einstein was not born in Africa. She was hatched in California. Einstein's owners could tell that she was extra smart. That's why they named her after the scientist Albert Einstein. He was so smart that people called him a genius!

The talent scout drove over to meet Einstein. *Would she be as brainy as her namesake?* He hoped so. The breeders introduced him to Einstein. Einstein turned her head this way and that. Then she said a few words to him. That's right—she spoke!

All African gray parrots can mimic sounds. But not all African grays choose to do so. The scout could see that Einstein was naturally chatty. She would be easy to train. He took her to the Knoxville Zoo to try her out for the show.

Parrot Primer

Let's talk parrots:

- There are over 350 types of parrots in the world.
- Parrots usually live in tropical areas. But one type (above), the kea (sounds like KEE-eh), lives in the snowy mountains of southern New Zealand.
- Most parrots are brightly colored. Macaws (sounds like muh-KAWS) are some of the most colorful.
- All parrots have curved beaks.
  - Most parrots eat seeds and fruit. Some eat flowers and bugs.
  - Parrots have four toes on each foot. Two toes point forward and two point backward.
- The biggest parrots are the macaw (left) and the large cockatoo.

The trainers at the Knoxville Zoo put Einstein in her new home. They knew that like some people, parrots can be afraid of new places. But Einstein wasn't an ordinary parrot. She was curious. She checked out the parrot cage. It was big enough to hold a couple of large dogs. She saw that it had several perches, or branches. It also had three bowls. One was for water. Another was for food—berries and seeds. The third bowl was empty. Soon Einstein would find out what it was for.

In no time, Einstein made herself at home. Zoo trainers put toys in her cage. They gave her shiny beads to play with. They gave her bells to ring. Sometimes they hid food inside tubes. She liked to figure out how to get the food out!

It didn't take the zoo long to decide that Einstein would be good in the show. But she had to be trained. Scientists say that African grays are as smart as five-year-old children. But they behave like two-year-olds. That meant Einstein had a lot to learn.

Teresa Collins became her first head trainer at the zoo. Teresa knew the first thing Einstein needed to learn was to trust her. So she dropped treats into the third bowl in Einstein's cage whenever she walked by. Sometimes she tossed a peanut into the treat bowl. That was the best. Einstein loved peanuts! Einstein soon learned that Teresa made good things happen.

After a while, Teresa tried something new. Instead of dropping a treat into the bowl, she pinched the food between her fingers. She held it out to Einstein. African gray parrots have strong beaks. Teresa wanted Einstein to take the food gently. Einstein had learned that Teresa was her friend. She knew better than to bite the hand that fed her.

One day, Teresa put her hand into Einstein's cage. She hoped Einstein would climb onto it. It would mean that Einstein trusted her. Trusting a human can take time, so it's a big step for a parrot. But not for Einstein.

Did You Know?

Sometimes African gray parrots will shrink the pupils in their eyes, bob their heads, stretch their necks, and throw up. It's a sign that they love you!

Want to know what happens next? Be sure to check out *Parrot Genius!* Available wherever books and ebooks are sold.

INDEX

Boldface indicates illustrations.

MORE INFORMATION

To find more information about the animal species featured in this book, check out these books and websites.

Nic Bishop Snakes, Nic Bishop, Scholastic, 2012.

Snakes in Question: The Smithsonian Answer Book, George Zug and Carl Ernst, Smithsonian Books, 2004.

"How Titanoboa, the 40-Foot-Long Snake, Was Found," Guy Gugliotta, Smithsonian.com, http://www.smithsonianmag.com/science-nature/ how-titanoboa-the-40-foot-long-snake-was-found-115791429/?no-ist.

Animal Diversity Web, University of Michigan Museum of Zoology, "African Rock Python," http://animaldiversity.ummz .umich.edu/accounts/Python_sebae/.

National Geographic, "Animals: Green Anaconda," http://animals.nationalgeographic.com/animals/reptiles/ green-anaconda/.

Woodland Park Zoo, Seattle, "Indian Rock Python," http://www.zoo.org/sslpage.aspx?pid=1942#.U7MUIKgRzoB.

Woodland Park Zoo, Seattle, "Reticulated Python," http://www.zoo.org/sslpage.aspx?pid=1949#.U7MT7agRzoA.

This book is dedicated to my dear friend Joe Slowinski, who dedicated his life to studying snakes and sharing his passion for these often misunderstood animals. I like to think that some of Joe's passion rubbed off on me. When it comes to snakes, I owe Joe everything. —B. B.

CREDITS

Cover and all interior photos are courtesy of Brady Barr unless noted here: 9, Mike Raabe/Design Pics/Getty Images; 16 (UP), ZSSD/Minden Pictures; 16 (LO), Ch'ien Lee/Minden Pictures; 25, Nick Garbutt/naturepl.com; 33, Bruce MacQueen/Alamy; 40, imageBROKER/Alamy; 49, John Cancalosi/NationalGeographic Creative; 59 (UP), Barcroft Media/Getty Images; 59 (CTR), Wil Meinderts/Buiten-beeld/Minden Pictures; 59 (LO), Philippa Lawson/naturepl.com; 65, BSIP SA/Alamy; 72, Michael D. Kern/naturepl.com; 83, A Giant Sea Serpent by French School (16th century); Bibliotheque Nationale, Paris, France/The Bridgeman Art Library; 88, E. R. Degginger/Alamy; 97, Picture Collection, The New York Public Library, Astor, Lenox and Tilden Foundations; 101, Knoxville Zoo; 102, Knoxville Zoo; 106 (UPRT), Andrew Walmsley/NPL/Minden Pictures; 106 (LOLE), James Steidl/Shutterstock

ACKNOWLEDGMENTS

A big shout-out goes to all the scientists working on snakes who let me tag along on their research expeditions in swamps, deserts, wetlands, mountains, rain forests, woodlands, bogs, and marshes all over the world, and who so patiently taught me all they know about the wonderful animals we call snakes. Also, to all the snakes out there that let me get up close and personal with them (excluding the one that bit me on the face) and help tell the world how amazing they are.